CW01574920

Ecem,

CALDEBROC

Thanks for coming all the way from London – good luck with future metamodernist writing!

Best Wishes,

'Tordhale Siche descending to Caldebroc, then to the pit near Preste Platteforde and then to another pit, then to the ditch of Roger the Clerk, then to the hedge of Richard the Rimeur, then following the hedge to Caldebroc.'

from F. R. Johnston,
Eccles, the Growth of a Lancashire Town (1967)

ANTONY ROWLAND

Caldebroc

Arc Publications
2023

Published by Arc Publications
Nanholme Mill, Shaw Wood Road,
Todmorden OL14 6DA, UK
www.arcpublications.co.uk

Copyright © Antony Rowland, 2023
Copyright in the present edition © Arc Publications, 2023
Design by Tony Ward
Printed by TJ Books Limited, Padstow, Cornwall

978 1911469 31 5 (pbk)

Cover image:
'One street in Manchester' © Colin Taylor
by kind permission of the artist

ACKNOWLEDGEMENTS

The following poems have been published in journals and magazines: 'Trane on Fifth', 'The English Cemetery', 'Salviatino' (the final two as 'The English Cemetery') (*Stand*); 'Manchester and Leeds – where are they?', 'Ponden', 'Oxenhope' (*The Fortnightly Review*); 'We sponsored September', 'Fred the Shred is Dead', 'When I am on Wall Street' and the first two sections of 'The Bingley Ripper' (*Blackbox Manifold*); 'Old Time' (*English*).

'Cring' and 'Strangeways' appeared in the 'Place 2020' section of the Centre for Place Studies website (as 'M31 Cring' and 'M42 Strangeways' in the 'Manchester' sequence), https://www.placewriting.co.uk. 'Marl' featured in the preface of *Metamodernism and Contemporary British Poetry* (Cambridge: Cambridge University Press, 2022).

This book is in copyright. Subject to statutory exception and to provision of relevant collective licensing agreements, no reproduction of any part of this book may take place without the written permission of Arc Publications.

Editor for the UK and Ireland:
Tony Ward

When the last visitor
brakes the frost
Howarth's grit box
settles into night
salting its boggart.
When the moors
were clubbable
and farms emptied
into post, before
the parsonage turned
into cloth, table sorcery
with auxiliary charts
attuned to zen. Sleighs
nod their repeat. Shutters
drop their cards
and clear a space

CONTENTS

WORTH

CALDEBROC

THE INVESTMENT MANAGER'S REPORT

URSWISK

THE THREE DEUCES

THE BINGLEY RIPPER

Worth

I 'Manchester and Leeds – where are they?'

after Elizabeth Gaskell, The Life of Charlotte Brontë

Sleuth-hounds pursue their money
and purse against the hoarfrost
the hale men lingering custom
spinning at the great wheels
until factories crash the dawn

Declivities tend to brutalise
the roads draining as sloop rinks
to magnates of secluded hamlets
where you stair to alter a pump
the bill as gel in your folding plans

Your crime was only a lock
dreaming of saddle-girths in mud
halting the precinct with a face
conducted under pressure, sizzling
above the pans of meat; your daze

He stays as a bastion of exactitude; lichen
blooms on slate like jellyfish crowns,
his silence rare as a vendace
where black clings as drainpipes
your stain blinked in his violence

The lithophones of Hornfels stone:
lark warble to the bass of a funeral
where we dream of mycologist and Herdwicks
volcanic tuff dropped in the mist
trust as belaying the fells' edge

Dangerous when perverted
I shall forget the utterance, the utter
indomitability of your palate
a glutton for banishment
among lords doting the parish

All doors open to winter
and the harshness of a wrong bun
loosen the table with a blessing
you meilly-mouthed larrups
singing the tun to Asketh bridge

Charms to endow the loom
cordial as mountains, gentle
as a vestry meeting, happy
for occasion, the scutter
of gimcracks in an alleged park

Norse-bred natives until cholera
peculiar forms of population, a race
sagacity and dogged power
as Chiserley pins the valley
to light crag, the deciduous sway

Affections are not wide-spreading
amenities of curt and tone
the blunt squalls and hill air
rough as this vinegar, the pane
freezing our drinker backs to mash

Turn the bar churl into Joseph
and enduring grudges, more leads
than wallets on this bloody loon
who still draws stone in his wallet
for debts that flit to a Halifax chain

Irregularity mars the pastoral
authority grumbles as a cur
the pedigree enters to lap
grapefruit of a Goose Eye pot
the dye turning the streams to beat

Lamartine, Kossuth and Dembinsky:
replies crust to an insult. Doited,
the youths warch in their blood
to skunk among the rivers' leaves
skilled to an ordinary yes

Ancestral homes are a dense thaw
among the becks and minerals
arvills pitched between mourners
where we now rub a cottage bed
half-naked and blooded as a foot-race

Psalms flog the church mornings
of Norse ancestors who repair the Bull
as respect, stored with cold possets
and the dog's nose of chased ale: shirk
your liquor and face a pawsing

Hardening as mint cake, the people turn
addle and die among the sumphishness
of fire hogs, the defibrillator hung
as relic by those panting over stamps,
the wreck divining the branches

Strangers came from beyond Burnley:
finial teeth lodged their slate
their box a lintel punched with crosses
their clouds weigh on Widdop tarn
carts distort the angled panes

Servants rubbed his circulation
to great raptures, the third heaven
a sermon lasting Lent, with fervour
of Wesley in as many churches per acre
as these pubs wrapped in winter bights

Stone the football to pebbles
challenge the alternative parish
to moor races; say neigh
to profligacy under the bare moon
for a chapel bolstered to element

Arvills and the foot-races
pitched the mourners to froth
the railway ales from India
pale as a citrus to ruddy
these dogged cuppers meld to fire

Not enough room for communicants
pray do not flatter them at Hell
with their eyes open to seed-cake
everyone inattentive to knees
among gems elusive as a bit-coin scam

Do not walk between service fields:
he sports a whip to the public houses
he flogs the loiterers to genuflect
we push our lungs on his cobbles
mounting our inklings to breath

You awaken those to God
snivelling in a backwards room
you nobble with a raw onion
we press the space with Espace
an incline jaded to a pad

The horse-races were objectionable
combustible to wickedness
tea scones busted with currants
by a stream enhanced with liquor
a stone cross bought to its please

He brought his earnestness
rain buckets that spurned the feast
no beast or footing for a man
the faithful ministration of a pint
the peeled virtue of HEART AND SOUL

Revenge as hereditary duty
among the heavy grasses and poor moss
wrong in Lawrence, alleviate
our sump of black pudding, bloody
as the nose of the baker's trot

Thoresby prunes mourn the rosemary:
he was obliged to desist: they
beat him to the Keighley turnpike
we partied there after a hint
and rolled our thighs in tin potches

Give dissenters their kale through the reek,
back bites and sniggle. Dogs warm pelts
in the sotted aperture of The Fox and Goose
where a guitar unseats our pints
with its bend leather, greedy to palm

Ovver th' steyres you were,
the sty of a grouse's mizzle
sticking the doors of the chapelry
hunting to quaff the rigger
or the grapefruit of a pale Chinook

Rain intensifies the tiles
the deadening orange buoys
the swell of beans that need sticking
reminiscences that stand a pillow
SENTIMENTAL STATIONS WILL BE MADE

II Ponden

after Charlotte Brontë, Shirley

Jupon, camisole and curl-papers
as rocks and quicksands;
an improper fichu
opened to the blinds, and
a sunset parsing its cloud.

Echoes of the snatches:
the canker exasperates
over the uneven lanks
of Brontë water, the skylarks
shifting between practice falls.

Bring taste: dulcet creams
or the parkin rusks in cafés
like Villette: the black peas
of border towns where Haworth
pits into the outskirt heath.

The glebe-house as grave
in Peri-mask; a soft
agitation of space as we
join the hollow and kittle pots,
shuffling over the borders.

Tighten your skin to
a parson's 'fit' and girth
of chocolate surtout: a mud road
gunged with tyres, the grass
raising its edge to Ponden Mill.

A shillelagh grasped
in his dexter fist: random questions
for a shovel hat and sog pattens
where a lapwing quiff
crashes the path to Oxenhope.

The poet's festal brightness:
a Yorkshire burr bulls out
the ratton's squeak. Cuckoos impress
as merlins, then doves bend
in return to an errant V.

The steam of dye houses
repeats in a cloud shift:
prepare your lollies among
tea cloughs with heads
pitted against his metal darlings.

Buried in coeval oaks:
BD22 I could never believe
was a home outpost, pestled
between Thornton's confusion
and the iced reservoirs of Colne.

Uncorrupted excellence:
the musk of heated bookshops;
the clean pride of Mr Moore;
the pale ribbons of Stanbury
mugged in a sky of orcinol.

Wormwood and gall to Luddites:
the squatting mills
repel in selfish moonlight
up to the saddle girth
in their bloodied pitch.

Outrageously charitable
like dripping lard or
another larrup perquisite
over the cobbles to pot
the road jagging to Oakworth.

The double frills of a net-cap
surround the pulpit brow
now railings carted for shrapnel,
the cow parsley of kine,
paths of sycamore rainment.

A continual fry and beef slice
of parson invasion: cheese
coagulates your guttle like
rock pips bleeding their foam;
apples winnowed as choice pigs.

Let's settle the Dissenters,
your samel disciples
over the animal pitches
of uncaulked bone: they pace
and flume the cattle grids.

A shower of curates
horse the siling evening,
pool their fripperies
among the farms ripped
to blocks and beams of teeth.

Luddites build to a rush –
Mun we say, wisht! Lig down? –
as cow afterbirth beads
its string of liver, garlic
abacus and bulbing lungs.

Decidedly inclined,
the embonpoint at Fieldhead;
the Jacobins rich in dykes,
down in conifers trained to patch
dwelling toys on purple moor.

Crabbed contumacy
among the stickle of non-
resistance; this pipit taming
the path tributaries
of early bilberry greens.

Subject of panegyric:
his blood is good, coated
with these submarine hills
periscoped as forests, and
absent trails of Saxon barks.

I feared your loveliness
among the sides falling
to becks that sop the woods,
the moor edge of Enshaw
trawling its core.

Drink eagerly of lune, as
you waste your snow-wreath
after Tartar's fangs;
cling to your posset
and the flagging stone.

An eulogium of beech
slides the wide angle
of these beck valleys; stones
mossed and shed from
the lost hands and scattered pew.

Please be a vicinage
or bounteous repast beyond
the expostulation of lovely Harriet
as chickens bob the graves, Tabitha
mulled under a bricked swing.

The lake-lasses, een
that pierced a body through
hobble the tussock;
paths as white streams
and dry-stone as rampart.

You disdain sympathy
with a kindled eye, under
the heavy ashes
and clouds ranking
to your bonnet-point.

Girn at your perverseness
and despotic necessity
of ruling the clefts: you
are parched for an answer,
tucking into its afternoon.

Your nose flasks a strand
among the doddered oaks
as morning spreads its poppies
to corner folds, slowing
the boulders' approach.

Wise in precocious conceits
is Jessie's cuckoo-song;
all these participles
cranking the past to
a willow-patterned tureen.

Mounds of sullen outline
beyond the jessamine lattice,
the pencilled shadow
of a church hunkering its dead
and filling its gates.

III Oxenhope

after The Letters of Charlotte Brontë

A crude rhapsody of tilt
and leaf: paper quires
run to sand, and books
grass a lost exhibition.
A gin-ring races

a circuit to Gomersal
and Cleckheaton where
a reservoir frowns its laps.
Done up with prosing
and charivari art stew:

cuckoo still imitates hawk
where becks teem the scud
in Chapel Plat and mud brooks
the colour of quaigh
or usquebaugh under cottages

boxing their grimestone.
Boli of turf blacken
like Warren's jet;
follow the pipit thrill
to Ogden spores

after the flesh farewell
of Ash Wednesday. Your
Schwester mourns as wires
rust the current
under the eyes of side-

jaw to cud: stunned
with opium, the reeds
flatten like a brother's will,
a cloud away. Hydropathic
establishments in Ilkley

are fogged to the Batley
corn mills where clitter
runs to sphagnum
and a collie holes
its frisbee in a ramrod

declivity: cry the family
into soap. Fern browns
to wind slant and moss
spreads the northern bark.
Light shales the back surface,

not a portal geography, but
nearly couched eyes, cut
after The Salutation slub
and cataracts as deep
as a gulph of verge

in sackcloth weather
when rain circles
an intolerable thaw, tight
as a charley horse
on the vicarage in Oundle.

IV WORTH

Your legs appear in front
as cables phone the ridge and
an old rose slurs its calyx.
Odd pulses light the settling.

Moors – half-seas turning wind:
an oystercatcher revs its chirr;
casts its alarm miles down-sand
to creeks twisting their nerve-ends.

A house presses the crop
where a canopy burns to mint.
Pied lapwings outwit the carrion;
piper and egg away from nests.

Isolate the crested field:
sycamores beach the cleft
where stonechats offer their throats
and a twite mobs the hovering.

Through the lattice to repast:
humble the path scions
and stick to the mud scar
where a redstart hides the drip.

Redolent of the stable,
Top Withins copes its trash
with dry-stone pockets.
We mire the walking shoots.

Emetic sandwiches glue their flies.
Thorn-caught: remedial bleeding
swills the nerves to passage.
Clouds jerrycummumble blue.

Mim pipits pick our edge
of crumb-shuck cheddar.
Gorge on a six-mile pan where
nimbus threatens its termagant.

Imagine the rough surtout,
a pertinacious thrust where
ramblers exchange their miles
with lugubrious stonework.

Rabbits snook us as lubberly
while a cloud-snag buffets
Laneshaw Bridge. Steeples
cut the pine to daw.

Grouse skitter the pass
like tractable thoughts.
Blandishments crumble
in our asperity's wake.

Picaresque as The Grot,
loosed stone gives to board.
Diagrams point to the station
like Pennine imputations.

Forgive bap peccadilloes
with exercise catechisms.
We lumber the moss
back to Laithe water.

Your flask is an empty husk
of conjugal endearments.
Curlews delay their whirr
then mourn our passing.

v Last of the Weavers

Still and grained as thackstone, you
salt down for winter use
and twill the lightweight shalloons

then suspend the fire, remember
carding into rollags, your youth
hammering wool to a fulling-mill,

raising the fibres on tenter-frames
to a teazle head, while the comb-pot
fed its semolina under pad nebs.

Now you flay the flaights of turf
for the colon hearth: nothing higher
than your delf until the Urals.

Gales theak the slate; iron pintles
hang the crop, and your future
where an ogee moulds the ashlar cap

and quoins stop to a rubble kist.
An egg-pan and riddleboard
spit their oatcakes as you grave

the earth after a mattock; pull
summer and its hay lazins tight
with a half-hitch. Blaeberries

ripen to your bowl: you skenk
the milk into a cream pot, skimmed
with blue for Stanbury meal.

Your oath is a curdle with keslops
into muslin vats, a panderwaff,
as you pig in bed with relatives

adjoining the loom. The thible
doles porridge. More oatcakes
foam the baxton, where loom wood

makes a dull plunge against
all black factories, a heck to weave
the last hopsack selvedge.

The last weaver, a right ravel coppin,
pushes his bothy stick on
the turbary road that served the pit

to Alcomden Stones – glaciers
that snavelled to tor.
Apron boulders sledge the hill.

The last weaver breathes the lines:
Stanbury pops the Eustachian
and grass moguls warp the fall

to Securiplex huts. Lichen
feathers the stone where sheep cud
at bullace stops. Courtesy

sets off in Back Lane; a lark
accelerates its last moment
where rams chew their blood.

The last weaver's mind laiks
in the hearth of a dairy sink
sunk in the milch-fold, cracked

with an arched lintel; quoins
that close the path to Crumber Dike;
a marine band of iron pyrites

that underpin the fireclay pits
at Benty Hole. Fools dug the beck
for Stanbury gold, ferrous sulphate,

from delf scars mined to burnt crop.
Drystone caterpillars to ledge and
grouse thicken almost to bleat.

Caldebroc

i.m. Kieran Crump Raiswell (1994-2013)

i Swinton

Egil's violence hones its drill
where a candle dries to a spat
in *Swynton*, a *tun* that banked its river,
now a marina coated with tench,
a culvert stack and landfill tipping.
You should be passing edges: instead
your passing anniversaries run
in this tun *pen* and Celtic *burh*.
A white bicycle prints the lane
as chalk; the bridge disappears
as traffic flack in Wardley. Crashed
forsythia an evening bulb:
skunk clings to Roots Night leavers,
their livers fighting like shrapnel
where the light sticks on Raby Street
and yellow cameras watch the night.

II Mosley Common

'A God-forsaken place, full of drunken, rude people with deplorable morals' (The Earl of Ellesmere)

The beech leaves soot and mellow as
a village welcomes cotton for death
in the bell pits of navigable levels.
Sticks pollute to Coccium,
shuttle with Starvationer boats:
the moat, iron oxide and leet
still orange the water and shale
in the *denu,* valley, shallow
as the coal seam of Grundy's field
where Kay's stirks bellow the pasture.
Cast an appropriate drapa:
Bennett Brothers craw and suspend
freighting bricks from Chine and Maersk;
flat bones expose the motherboard
of contemporary space. For HOME,
follow gas binders and anticlimb paint.

III CALDEBROC

And Uberisation under
acute-angled cranes; nacreous clouds
of Workedele, Quicklewicke, Swynhul
where chimneys stake their heritage
in the ditch of Clerk and Rimeur hedge.
Wireless trains download their scorn
as blackbirds distinguish tree bags
among perennial knawel.
Track arteries to your pitch
and lean, unforgiving shale,
melancholic economy
looping to your back pack; beyond.
Your plum tree is waiting for life:
tram cables tune to mist
where platforms moss to erasure
and container flats glass the arc.

IV CRING

Glazebrook to Stockport Tiviot:
a switching station burns the spur
where Shell refines its polythene
and air distils into fractals.
A mosque opens its journalist:
the roads are closer to us now,
tied by an event and tape
that breezes. Our bunches drift
around the statue. Anne buses
end in fresh streets as the sunshine
feints its relevance and sirens
inject their caffeine: yellow bibs
promote corners and match the smiles'
acid on bedroom walls. Trams
adjust their pitch along stations
where cube artists buckle their scrap.

v Dinton Street

Beast so cold that the milk chunked:
death is not a screen but the pleats
of your curtain, salmon, calling
the stalks. Ivy pinks the dead
trunk in this antioxidant month:
teeth gravel crunches our stomachs.
Braille caps sweat the bridge rivets
and the tram's middle accordion
gasps our path to your Candlemas:
we pat the casket as relic,
lip bits and perishing finish,
too dry for sandwiches: oak me;
I will never score you again.
Flakes offload their offering
as trail lamps bobble the Irwell
and the Waterwomble trawls its scrap.

vi Norwegian Freeze

The clocks are down. You spread the night.
Manchester rain: a trashed windscreen
ices the lot. Cumulus steaks
bargain their red among the slate
and I have forgotten your time
of life and date in The Chophouse
where Skin-hood, father of Kalf,
keels to the Christmas market.
Romsdal, Ancoats, Jamtland: measures
have been taken against outrage,
derring-do amongst sausages
and the onions burned to sweet.
Snakker du engelsk, vaer så god?
Skin-hood's invisible *reinsdyr*
echoes the wood as I raise
guilt, and an impotent pint.

vii Madam's Wood Pits

A displacement lubricator
bears the axle and the Roscoe valve:
mine spoil freights to Cutacre tip
and Clough dumps from the Brackley line.
Walkden steams the collieries: now
rework history to amenity,
woodland, wetland and overspill.
This is a strategic area:
Pound shops are broken; GOD AS NEW
CANCELLED in the Dun Mare's breeze.
CCTV as Tardis bulb:
barbed wire apportions the drop
for the last Swan out of the box.
Sky a muckied ticket before the sile:
Laxardel in Little Hulton;
clouds pelt and sicken their red.

VIII POTATO WHARF

Panto is over, thank Twanky:
winter's first sand grips the edge
as yellow nooses move the beat
of the fishplate, splice bar and trams
create our pavements, lapped
with waves of tar. This is not fare:
cobbles like kidneys gloss the dawn
and a cable's strop disturbs
the air. You have botched
the parameters, this year
as coasters are taken elsewhere
and memory shrinks to a circle.
Parallel lines hobble the kerbs
and hardhats turtle cable boxes
as the low sun pinches the heave,
fog solid to a clothing dump.

ix The Stretford Beef

Kieran sails across barges
to his Sale club and days of runs
where Porkhampton swilled its people
famous for buttered pig with sage
onto the *straet*. Across the ford
where the Traffords bossed the crossing
at Crossford Bridge: Bonnie Prince Charlie
and his army trough to London
and commandeer the rhubarb,
pink regiments of 'Stretford Beef',
flush as the Art Deco Essoldo.
Odeon: old cash-register
with pillars of phallic stamen,
stepped convex surfaces curving
upwards and backwards to advance
TOP RANK until the bingo freeze.

x Triassic Sale

Your innings anchors the outfield:
the runs keep with your splayed stumps
on the road from DEVA VICTRIX
to MAMUCIUM. Sale, *salh,*
golf lodge and vacated dovecote
of the old manor and night-soil boats
coated with the Bunter.
Drift geology of gravel
and sand at Broad Ees Dole
where geese hiss at the sallow tree
and cottages weave garthweb,
horse flax for saddle girths –
until the railways grind their halts
over canal packets and turnpike trusts.
The toll booth will soon be drive-in;
the intermittent pub, a totem.

XI DENTON HEADSTOCK

'If you want to get ahead, get a hat' (old Denton saying)

Measures against outrages:
butter and tin for an errand,
an amulet clot in Nico ditch
where Egil strops his violence. This
is Dane-town, *denu, daenland,*
where mercury separates fur
from hide and trilby. Hatter-mad
out of nitrate after curing
the Attaboys, but not the hands
as temperatures rise to pot
with sliver glands. Sot vapour
and methylated explosions
for soft, stiff, velour and wear.
Hard felt, the hat felt recession.
NO TAMPING on detrainment ramps:
redacted walls now paste their black.

XII JWM-018

This station walks with Mamba: do
not elbow out the trance or shivers
by the ticket machine. Rails
jam the passengers' heads, screened
on reflection: a man enters
his Spice and then moves the platform,
jittering his silence as leaves
begin their ribs with branches scraped
like rosemary at Failsworth Pole.
The flyover connects its vacancy:
routed tight as a necker
and poem, your diversion scouts
close birches that yellow the north
of Daisy Nook, dibbing the nav
into high roads, synthetic hills
taut for the siren and mambulance.

XIII SMEDLEY

A mind like an empty salad:
mornings inject, cannabinoid.
Stubborn as buddleia, they rise
with fiscal burden as just rage.
Brexit – depot entry only:
touch-out at the Firswood spur
or Pomona's skerry; slow eyes
to a passing sign or a sliced blond
in the ear mirror. BEWARE
OF RAIL: tipping jackdaws
toe Collyhurst and its blown dunes,
equator-flit into Sandhills,
'a goodly quarre hard by town.'
Rufous moon, we grease the night
in the Electric Circus, where
a trebled bass plies its joy.

xiv Ducks

Chilled in outer Duckinfield,
we dress with the heat of spiders
on a returned postage stamp
of a boundary, wicket to wick.
The changing room is a webbed plank
and playground trellises are plagued
with our opposition's slogs.
Beaten, we still survive that dad
boiling by the rope expletives.
In your penultimate season,
cherries flower the frost
and lawnmowers sulk their cuts.
Our failure in innings
will always be our own; that day.
Clouds sting the April tail between
the cars tearing from a cracked strip.

XV THE BLUES TRAIN

(Granada TV, 1964)

Scrambled eggs was chicken too, when
The Blues Train stationed at 'Chorltonville'.
One goat wallops in a tether:
white folks chew their harmonicas
and pick in the station, beatniks
nodding to a cantor. Unlike
the lone black conductor who rolls
to frame, bored as the credits. I
could look a cold dog in the face:
Muddy's slide mimics steel and frets.
Didn't it rain, gospels Sister Tharpe
to the sun's impeccable hiding
on a railway path you biked, happy
as a Chopper. Now balustrades
vanish into dock patch, balsam
where Egil mugs with his bike pole.

XVI The Polled-Cow Verses

'I think the sooner the trolls take you, the better'
(The Saga of the Confederates)

Mersey – contested boundary
between Poicton and Saxon Edin:
motionless clouds step their light
and the kingfisher's blade hums.
Entrenched to the Ribble, our torches
middle January's depth. Leaves
pace the grass. We plough our steps:
an upended ash roots its question.
Laces are worming their eyeholes
in our mercenaries' bitten feet.
I can only lick sleep, due to
earlier verbiage, the usual
leaders' trot. Yet, we are so close
I can feel the pear. We dream
over the ocean to Hop, and
a bright staying with the whitings.

XVII Strangeways

The evening falls to a burst string:
a hung audience smokes its cool
as rain exits to bouncers' hands
and a Fender feeds the shutter,
an open chord into the white
where Strangeways towers its closure.
The Arms empties to a wolf moon:
red lights carry the silence, and
our fear settles the fog, exposed
as your voice, softer now,
on a footbridge threatening a map.
Cans beach the Irwell, and canned
factories press to yellow cones
that spell our night. Planes outwit
the stars. Count four to orchestrate:
our scrapped bars jenga the lot.

The Investment Manager's Report

I We sponsored September

for Alan Greenspan (1926-)

Dice as indices rarely cite the vendor:
this table is commonly used to provide aid
in your asset class as reality blooms
like a pupil into understanding:
historical analysis is a forecast, but
you must assume the entire risk to predict.
We disclaim all warranties of originality,
accuracy, completeness, timeliness
and non-infringement of a particular purpose:
Wall Wall Wall Wall – to me that's a holy place.
Do not accept errors or omissions:
we sponsored September, and it peaked;
after that, mounting material polished its sell off
while investors overwhelmed the overview –
listen oh gold pipes to this Archimedes
squinting at the mirror like an equity market,
buzzing in geopolitical issues and tissues
winding the fizzing blood of trained concerns.

Smack it through liquidity into light
and the chundering tongue – uncancelled debt.
Jerome Powell suggests a hit, a line
of pumice stone as his hawkish comments
grew a sleeve: party with this sponge;
sell off November to the technology sector
amidst concerns about hope, implemented
in an ever-widening China where major banks
continue creeping their foamy edge.

Polish your globes into waxy moons
and pressure the oil into plunging food:
quantitative waning lowers its rose.
Brexit works towards the UK's resignation
as the market plunged October into May;
volatile as August, equities risked a douche
and peak that fell into excessive fiction.

Bring down the target to sentiment
and oil me with the most unguent perfumes
when Truss erodes the polls to power base:
robust as a tight Germany, GDP!
Towel a dovish boost to prompted gains
as apace China steams its measures
fuelling the effect of a worries stem
after the rupee discounted the Pacific
and the Nikkei index hit a bellwether
and sold October for Japanese steel,
but the yen was weaker against a balloon
so slow down tit-for-tat to a bleak backdrop:
China can fall as well as rise; a policymaker
who proposes the overseas to the past and
emerges into a settlement with the mini-bar
at the time of a custody of securities, at
the level of a target guaranteed to emerge.

Manchester Metropolitan University

Manchester Poetry Library

Manchester Poetry Library

Give us your feedback and recommendations

Write your thoughts below and hand this card back to a member of staff

Visit mmu.ac.uk/poetrylibrary
poetrylibrary@mmu.ac.uk

II Fred the shred is dead

for Fred Goodwin (1958-)

An accompanying table of asset class
aids your understanding of the provided vendor
indices, cited as a magnitude performance:
sterling performance, Sterling. This
is a commonly used calendar year sports return;
though magnitude does not constitute advice,
and the source for your internal use
may not be reproduced or disseminated
in a form or basis. Do you
think monkeys give? Let's all
slope cabinets to shuck others' mess. Always
refrain from making historical data
since analysis should guarantee risk;
after all, the user informs on affiliates,
each person merchantability without purpose,
but please do not pursue my family: do you
have any punitive, incidental consequences?
Use permission to distribute without approval:
copy Russell footsying the FTSE,
dripping with a data vest. We
do not endorse the content, written consent, but
enjoy the momentum of a subdued Canada
and emerging concerns – tightened liquidity
or the Chinese fall on material omission. Do
not take the sword off this banker-knight. Write
a dollar-denominated trade feed, providing wind
and a head stand-off escalation, higher tariffs
on an ever-wider range of bachelors. Bray
the qualitative tightening: the Fed

guided hikes through the remainder, the valley
in which England rates the gradual. Terminate
the autumn and replace with the Bank of Japan
to water all your asset-purchase, and clip
the temptations (bond-buying programmes): prune
oil that floods to a three-year high. Bucket
the inflation remains; bonfire the unchanged rates.
How can a man live on three million a year?
In Europe, political uncertainty breaches limits
with sentiment after Johnson lag lag lagged
and slowed to a robust June. Flowers
are unlikely to fall to the unemployment rate
but keep cats' eyes on impressive forecasts:
chicken the storm while I eye some golf.

European markets did announce the Swedish,
didn't they? But Italy was weaker, bonded
to pick indicators, quarter and flash
as unemployment tested the unity: unnerved,
investors picked a fight with Genoa;
the bridge collapsed to a unit test. I
had a plan to radically boost political development:
deadlock, no-deal, Brexit entrenched
and led technology like a bear driver,
liking its basis to first America, raised
to an insinuation and a fake aide, dimming
the dispute between Korea and a shift.
You turn my house into an omelette,
the historic bleating emanating from a shadow
that alleviated the partner year Ung.
Japan unsettled us with the Philippines.
Stem the aggregate of denomination!
Auntie Abe rebounded into scandal and
favoured decline over deepening warrants

although personally the BoJ targeted
the 'tit-for-tat' January peak market,
June-locked between the yuan:
pension me with your manufactured love.
Caixin deteriorates to a curb;
leverage on a clamp-down release
peaking into a blind quarter part comp.
Clamp down on excessive exposure: any views
are subject to change without notice;
we no longer accept new information.
If you have not matured, pend your instruction.
If you have less, use a telephone. If
you'd like to withdraw proceeds, stop reading.

iii When I am on Wall Street

for Philip Gramm (1942-)

'Some people look at sub-prime lending and see evil. I look at sub-prime lending and see the American dream in action'
(Philip Gramm, 2001)

Please bail out our help-life: trade
with recipients acting on contents; the vendor
is class. Time plane: a non-infringement
on timeliness; rally on a pop umbrella.
Historical data provided as an 'as is' basis
with the underlying party contained
in your sponsors. Do not endorse
the content of this communication: global
earnings overlook low volatility, turbulent
as a robust globe, the status quo
of banks reversing a loose Fed. Taper
your balance sheet to fuelled headwinds
while I plonk a castle in your data,
rubber flutters like pennies inflating
my blue situation: so many punters
and bathers despoiling the bonds.
What a performance! A drive flashes
in a Riviera weave, commodity
splices that benchmark your courage:
your money sandpapers its own wad
in a quarterly Brexit. Sharp
as equity, Richie dangles a retainer.
The beachball was a difficult issue:
our target risks tailed January
so neck a rubber cocktail now or
the record high of a job, decisions

where my sand-feet turtle the bands.
Steward into the leeward picture,
the core energy of a massive bailout:
make that a bubble, lathered in sterling.
A calendar of magnitude constitutes advice
and higher prompts in a sell-off rally:
I wrap your accounts into news
and lick the indices, spade turn, asset, but
Korea enjoyed a double-digit return,
slinking index bars as metal tariffs.
Tick inflation to a rout: every dollar
fluctuates its exposure, a fly slip
to your edgy predicaments, as I
sweat into an expat banister, barred
from managing your preparation, switched
between the rise of a hot belly, retired
into sand crust and the forecasts of daiquiri.

Urswick

i.m. Richard Thomas Jones, 1972-2018

i Burrator

You are entering a different poem:
first chemo's fluff to even skin
where ointment replaces the hormone fuzz.
The cutting evens with trees: you laugh
at funerals in a culvert
as minerals juice the navvies' stone
and fall in copper water to the hand
of a saved month and a cuppa that cuts
through damaged buds. Spring offends:
the wagtail's yellow mints a bench
where we mumble through our lunch.
This is not a cancer poem:
relieve the mud with a warbler's turn;
tree-boot echoes into Tamar sludge.
Our children once bulbed in the pit,
then poddled to the sand, tors and
pebble-cairns as your distant pills.

II Marl

'Dr Jones was a physical geographer whose research at this tarn and elsewhere around the world added greatly to knowledge of the Holocene.' (Urswick tarn memorial stone)

Herons stumble the fetch: Urswick
holds its flash, setting the tarn
with our wake, appropriate
as our grief through laughter, where grass
spikes the meniscus and sun-motes blur
our digital snap. Hug
the embarrassment of this plaque:
mourning as clear as fish that roll
air and under the boardwalk. We
taste the edge of marram, faces
in all-shore directions; eyes
string the reed buntings jittering
their pad. Marl adds
to our knowledge of the Holocene:
your core sampler hods to pollen
where forests mould to a crick
and insects peat our memory. Grain
fires the cap to a dating spree.
Photos out-tilt the jetty's pitch, as
we walk out in our guilty retrieval.

III OLD TIME

You laugh into vision in Amsterdam
as a wasp bulbs my lip to vinegar,
stung-drunk among the mayonnaise,
and a library ferments to a cheese store
by Bijenhof, where Nazis banned the ties
from soldiers mouldering under the clock,
piers, lintels and corbels that tower
BEIDT UW TIJD, bide DUUR UW UUR,
and delay our way to Café Mack
with Verwey's poem for us vreemd.
Shram bobs the gracht. A ro-ro checks the swell
where Chet Baker tunes to a ramp:
'You said, I said' foments in Oudezijds
Voorburgwal. I do not think
I actually could spare ribs. Chet
was not trumpeted among the throng but
relax: Lugano rafts wind the pedalos
and houses obey and adjourn into form.
Richard: a sausage roll calls your honour
as the electric silences its creep. Do –
as Verwey insists on the Beurs van Berlage –
our feats really happen at the proper *tijd*?

iv Crabbing

Side peeler:
a bucket of crumbled thoughts
knitted to pincers
and a stitch brow
submerging a pebble bob
to stalks sand dollars
barnacle urchins
mesh bait line weight
your chicken
plumbing the moment,
first fish
to your plenty.

Spider deeps:
they are pulling
all the grockles
clanking the fret
tagging their lag
lumping the Irish Sea
to insect crustaceans
tern sandbags
all mandibles intact
to whelk shells
chapped with
your last ink.

v The English Cemetery

No entrance guards the Florence nun:
CLOUGH battens in Chiavi, and
LANDOR needles the only sign.
A rose clue only to E.B.B.,
anonymous on entasis columns.
Flinch at the pottered graves
on the way to famed marble;
sign before attending the vinca
and lupin pots that fade the heat.
Leeds packaged the sick to climate
before the swamps provided the dead:
ANNE ails in the bake, before
her bite. Hunslet Presbyterians
rocked by their black churches
spread in the heat, pinned
by the Grand Tour's April *départ.*
I can only saccomazzone
to whip your traces like a blind pinata.
HOLMAN-HUNT bought melancholy
whereas the mercury celebrates
in this grave island, belted
like feet in its outsized gravel:
only Fiats peek the edge
and water is plastic to drain
in this grid system of hills
that part before our BROWNING.

VI SALVIATINO

Climbed near and then lost you
on the beeline skyline, Salviatino,
from where the Duomo and Vecchio
peak to jet. A garden line
hangs my balance in Vernon's patch
and the vines' resentment: even shade
overheats; I'm seeing this
for you. The marble huntsman
drawls his patch and the Christs
glow. Unrope the marble
on a hewn Neptune, lined with apricot
where unsurfaced fish circle
their depth and the fountain keeps
your fact. The Isolotto
limes to fruit: you follow me
as statues harvest the underground.
Ilexes point to opposite, bocage
terracotta houses, heaving with paint.
Cypress rides are stopped with olive
but vinca still bosses the top
as a lizard flicks to Ilex shadow.
The verge signals its unknown
and the rondo pants to censure
beside curtail roads that daze the set
while steps cut the baking loops to height:
Santa Croce sinks to range and my rage.

The Three Deuces

I Miles and the Third Bill

An apple crucible sands
the chord of 52nd Street:
bebop halters the gas skiffs
fresh from Minton's Harlem
hop; hip trunks square
the lighters and fill
the heat between
the Three Deuces,
Onyx and the diners
thick with omelette.
Fleet obbligati tune
rubberlegs, odd clinkers
but not the fluff, tugging
the ear from the tonic,
diatonic, warm and legato,
cup mute to avoid
the done. The cats
are hung. That F sharp,
orgiastic, floats the heads
of St Louis dudes, pimping
for a fix. Hoods
beat you to an addict:
demoted chops, embouchure
fumbling a double tempo
over crowds sophisticated
as an armpit, drown
out the vibrato slurs,
half-valve, smeared
notes we cop like

chicken soup, strained
buildings, filling in
the zoning envelope
between nitrates straight
as Pegler's taps. The
tinhorns and chisellers
on escapes that zag
their usual backs, drunk
on West 77th Street where
a snare drum rimshot
dips into your fame.

II Trane on Fifth

'I didn't go far enough' (John Coltrane, 1960)

Death and the kiosk
are all that are close:
stoplight; there is no air
in this city but there
is breath, no
siddity in a coffee
marooned on Formica
bulging to hold,
diurnal as poison. Bend
from the line, quit
resolution: unlike
a painting, you must return
but too much roll and
snare if you bust. Just
out of peach on Fifth:
the piano underwrites
its hand, trilled to
reflection. Pedal me. Not
jax over the overheated
or stop when you've ticked
the notes. Rim bass
that weighs like bread;
finger to peg stretch in
this city's peck: cymbal
symbols assemble morning.
Three conversations and a lost bar:
scream reed held to
cream fruition and
reprise on a stick ringle.

Brittle without vibrato,
a trebled bass releases
slurs and drifts. Back
in: quieten
to chord where fingers
tremble around the left, just
before it locks: shriek
to hear. Ghost melody,
multiphonic evenings
in rooms that shift
false fingers
out of the dawn.

III QUIFF

'Yer at 170 – you dumb quiff – count!'
(D. Richards, *Evening Snow Will Bring Such Peace*)

Obscure: New York flattop or mohawk,
formerly a plastered lock, favoured
by the glengarries or forage caps
of soldiers soldering their slimy arcs
brewed by the eyebrows; unlike
the moustache-waxers, the quiff plasterers
of a dandy generation (Reagan's pastiche); not
the brothel creepers of ripped-up Teddies
and seats ransacked to grease – drainpipes
slicked on comedy knees – Hindi for slick
this *quoff* or *coiffe*, knight mail camp as protection
or Dutch *kuif*, the Japanese punch perm preferred
by Yakuza and Bōsōzoku gangs.
Bring forward a lock: 'We bloomin' well 'ave
to lop it orf, no hank', pranked Mr. Punch
maligning it as disfiguring; akin
to a puff or whiff of tobacco smoke
smote in Georgia or Detriot slang.

Clear: texturize with a decent salt spray
then Dean at the back; modernize
with an undercut or a tapered fade.
Today, the sinks are smiling with neck points:
pump down a grade, then dab around
to an arm cut, the combination
of a comb tuck and a black tunic
that marks this tottering repair. Diner chairs
steel their levers in an abjection of junk hair;

pastes and sprays line up their admonitions,
mirrors into a future head. Juicing
the fractions of disrepair, pomaded
within an inch of restoration, the quiff
hangs, dogged, hair cliff of Heathcliffe
and all outroguers, outrageous yet reposed,
an everyday aping of absent stars.

The Bingley Ripper

Trees across the valley moss their burning,
ink their reds and copper in an ashlar sky.
Our family's haul to Shipley Glen: boulders
like Easter statues roped from the glaciers
streaming from Elterwater or Great Gable,
dropped a throw from the Ferncliffe estate
and fairground smells ghosted with slot,
tarpaulins as sighs gutted in the autumn.
Dodge a hat and suck to your parting gob.
Walser a magnet for scrawl, itinerant cows,
parched beeches planing the rocks' edge,
smaller boulders hiding the thumbed gum
and fish paper greased transparent. They
always stood for something else: fumbles in
the cut, assignations on a cliff as dangerous
as a spangled Durex. Across the ivy valley,
NF brushed in a Dulux scrawl; LEEDS or
BRADFORD whitening the lower divisions
across the hopeless Aire. Lined with beams,
we nosed across a ridge, hit the Ilkley turn
where sound punctured the valley air.
Pocked cracks. An impossible green
dipping to beck and then following stone.
Silent – then a shotgun as admonishment.
Even the flags are quiet on Baildon's heath
in the pub's warning of its own cross. Kecks
are sanded on the wind-down to Salts: chin
past the unseasonal yet hanging lights
where our chips are straight to a mill, coat
drystone snow. A woodpecker grins its lice.

Bingley mosses. You feign gormless.
Gaskell: Brontës were sullen as glen peat,
friendly as a glacier, self-sufficient,
churlish, loving and laughing at nothing;
kind as stones no intervening could gauge.
Excommunicated villages magnet to pawn.
You climb eggs to flappitt Baildon and
ridge of Dick Turpin for a breathing pint:
the Aire valley airs its annual bull show.
Regional certainties: crocked bark for Plot;
cracked molars on the dunked parkin pigs.
Hoard your silence unless you harbour airs:
Sutcliffe benefits from custom, iron wills
chained to the past like mild, a raised choir
at night with the Sauceworks' lush Abide.
Canals barge cuts: Five Rise Locks stands
as gibbet over the culvert. Brazen as a view,
the cargo of commuter slickers, moaning.
Concrete bunkers offend with civic graffiti;
undercutting chimneys divide their stubs,
airing their circles. Bingley cobble warrens
empty to a river and game throttles.
Sutcliffe tries to follow in outcrop steps,
grandad's out-plates of mutton offal
elbowed from kitchens: your mum ladles
chicklins and tripe that stretches your guts.
Reet: parting the cow heels sucked to trot.
Cheek. Your dad screamed when his chin lit
with the boiling gravy. Fireballs chipped
the heights, drystone snows to light our kid.

Honley: kerbside ferns bruised their rust.
Valleys turned their light over empty farms
and hidden dips larched their fire. Water
suffed to a belched wheel. The east road
elbowed to summit: rocks altered to sedge,
roping the glacier sky. Holme Moss, mast,
tasked the valley, closer to the new moons.
The moor stopped on a harrier's ledge:
barbs plucked the wool where stunt clouds
paused away from shell-holes and LARRY.
Sundays were these brambles, Christmas
an over-lit kitchen and stubbed leaks,
blackberries juiced with spag as slugs glued
to their appetite. Slay blaeberries sluthered
in harvest, ligged out in a moor's promise:
our blagged plastic was spelt with autumn
splatted among palavers of nettle. Gardens
sank into autumn drop: we were daft tykes
spreading the moor with our fat bags.
Neighbours ripened diction: we gave a toss
on the tarmac stage. Bone idle. Toe pumps
tipped and threaded to a rapt assembly.
Humdinger shrub. Slang match as bunting.
Close yap. Bone scut of an acid blackbird.
Now the Lammergeier feeds its pitch above
the mast, cuts marrow in upland bleach.
Untagged, feathers splint to an alp retrieval:
it charges its spiral above the Derwent as
grouse lose their season to the law of six.
The roads are deafening to scald Holmfirth.

A road tilts farms stubborn as their valleys:
the sun treadles its moors. Rita's bedsit dips
to a viaduct: you slide your trade in cars.
Great Northern Street belches its irony,
elbows its cobble and under-echo to rope:
the sky's limited to Blue Lace, Yates'
tasked to heels. New Punjabi notices appeal
to the moon with data to flatten the case
among dotty calls, doting fame to a crank.
Clouds like pranks stunt the hilltops.
Punters begin the lorry trickle as rumours
crown the papers and Peter treads caution.
Women skirt a puddle. Christmas is over
like a limp toilet. Market nights drag. Snow
threatens as the moon glues itself, clean
from the moor. Helen puzzles over the road
spelt with her family's loss. Timber hides
the crack. Boots spot over embankment.
Her eyes roll to a stack. Asbestos winters.
In court, Peter spouts Zapolski nonsense as
he courts, ripens his voice piped to a treble:
bovine to the rapt jury, liberated in dock, he
slangs personable and stooges a double.
Evangelical about yourself, stripped into
your class, you feed lights, articulate pitch,
cutting immaculate, bleaching lies. Experts
grouse over dupe, violence, your Honour,
only after the sentence of an icy wife. You
gad about your shrine and time jury ears
into the plea, backed crime, a *verbatim* gap.

Chips fat as rascals after a maiden fifty and grubs of scraps larded with their own heat. A pig's head carted the sky over mid-off: stoned balconies whistled their flags. Home clad in black stone up the dip: we mooched among the night's glass fuzz, mossy khazi, pizzas out of reach on a mounted screen. Fan-maze to The Skyrack, bantering locals among Quarry punters, squared drinkers glaring the buds on lawns choked with sun when afternoon lazed its clinks, students coked into a table blazed with lager and voice-fizz of a Taps run. Swerved rounds as terraces spread like nerves. Back to clod, that recorded November, Boddington mud sucked the defenders into ghosted space. Ham right-back after a night with a clown, the air still tanged of club, burst into speed and we were the only souls in a shower outlined for dogs, hooked stalls wet with dysmorphic creams. Minutes' ice slides across the green, the suburbs' milk frozen on valleys to Kirkstall ruins. Army bag stopped the police: they searched whites and a misspent mouth, youth hanging on futures spread with singed change. Cantana attracted fans' canned adulation. Leeds relationships scratched over chance, looking for exits as if proof of failure. We shared early Bud and then our legs changed.

The stagnant case fattens its months: eyes
part the ground for furloughed murders as
police belts loosen for Xmas slack.
Kirkstall: fired like a pup in new tin, Peter
guns the engine to ease the frost. Patience
drains the sky to Arndale crowds. Wait.
You whistle at dashboard flow. Stone
copies headlights as you drag glass waste:
sharp railings grill the drivers. Students
outrage at the raffia blood: a Panda curses
Headingley foiled by a mitten. Blasted after
the siege: the cameras daze their flash;
barter stories hot for the line. Glare notes
proffer shocked sums. Upbraided hacks
anticipate rounds with the after-gaffer, fizz
of a scoop spreading like a den. Nerves
edge for weeks as the BBC records its grief.
Repeat: Jackie nights that ghosted the stop.
Smelt spells it out while Trevor dutches
courage and ditches qualm. Stall the streets:
warnings gum the men, reclaimed dusks
iced with defiance, punters as a stumble.
The Plaza freezes its screens with eggs: NO
MEN AFTER DARK whitens to bobbies.
Share links to press the spite. Blitz. Blokes
mouth their suspect: tapped Geordies drain
and leave; suspicions can a marriage.
Scratch over the cracks. Adulterate. Fathers
search their exits in hugger-mugger pubs.
Coupons nag wall-sheaf. You leg it to close.

L.S. LOWRY: daffodils shrug his mint.
Crossed at the chapel's park heart, brushes
cake in rain, brimming with colour.
Clogged to humility and leavened granite,
candle-wax pools and grits with leaf.
Brooches watermark where the urn stacks.
JOHN ALCOCK plotted his Vimy biplane
to Canadian dunes: he trapezed the wing,
plugged fuel and slicked emptying clouds,
oiled reflections on the Nauset coast before
he toasted Clicquot for a first Trans flight.
His white cross sabres the graves: now
teething stones gather his exploits, expose
history. An angel scrolled with your feats
rolls back to your rickety tub: your plane
bathed clouds; a propeller fired its mizzle at
a new-found land in fuselage and pump.
These lime trees jut to trail: cars worm
nouveau mud over to the Noonans' patch.
Railing-holes knocked out to copper-green
chew a plain bulwark filling to gravel.
Dispatched after a bender, GRETTON
published his gloom expenses, listed chips
cheap as the uni plates, dives in which
discarded floors stuck to the soul. Music
plugged its city into a trebled bass.
Southern Cemetery: MARTIN HANNETT
in this new wing, his Hamlet heart never
small enough for a sect. Katyn faces:
Russians wrangle officer deaths to the pine.

Cemetery geography: Peter plots his routes with non-conformist zeal. Sniffer of garage fuelled with regret, the back brick-crops slicking neglect with weed, Peter coasts Moss Side: workers cling to the road, toast bodies safe from white-rose murders. Crack on to stones that serve your loop: influenza stakes its post-war graves. Route to Jean, kerbing the Corsair that wipes its rain. Personable as lime, you moon to a patch beyond grave railings, adjacent to waste. Jean's promissory note should see the end but hawthorns rise to upbraid their spot. Stung bottles. He hammers a ring finger, piling into dream. Your thumb is a left. Dizzy from nowhere, the headlights skulk the tackle as a car guns, misses your inches. Bushes tangle to daffodil wreck, a body soaking the allotments. Peter waters his fear as reports fail and neglect your haunt, clogged with grass, bucked into leaf-hole where cars rat. No regrets among the jeers in Elland Road stands: fans bleet the police. You waggle your meat plate into business, flex glass and stick your worst, vomit among the browning. Trembling, you burn your togs in a shed, rubbished to a holder. Clues enough to convict: banks pull batch; the note is pinned to dry. The police notes are encircled with his ready-made herrings.

A levered plot-hole chokes its rosemary
that flanks with urns and attendant angels.
Grave Y745 splices clean as a Weetabix:
lopped cherubs waste a plot. Jackdaws oil
UNTIL WE MEET AGAIN and HUDSEN.
A comma ends KNIBBS: its cirriform line
ices his shore. The conformist lanes clock:
I look for you among the smart joggers
eyeing their swatch, open graves planked
with drench. Stocked with current, a crow
hangs its quill: rachis to the umbilicus, vane
to calamus, its end-feathers trail to MUM.
Tenders mesh this space as a garden slot:
burnt holly whites the script. Canned urns
bury their spots. Riotous ivy unhooks
snow-bole, a triage of headless angels. Milk
is posted for miracle water. You are hidden
in death, Jordan and Millward. A dandelion
bursts. My umbrella hangs its useless bat as
goldfinches practise their nagging churgle.
Stones chess around the cremated FITCH
with lichen: beached octopi branch yellow.
Xanthoria Parientina scales the elder and
monk's hood swells its lobes, itches at
nitrogen air. Open books jank the granite:
CHIM and CHIM. MARY PYE botched
her liver, a smoked-out lover, the flowers
that sour to a pavement kipper. Flipped,
graves separate letters, crumble meaning:
the grass stays to ungum its paupers' teeth.

An unprecedented hole in the public arena,
embarrassed with rich misinformation. Add
Yvonne thickening on grass for weeks,
reward wonga spliced with regret. George
is pinning a fevered map. He secretes Leeds
to a Henden centre that crashes on its data.
Red-light areas are minted with beak. Sonia
crosses your kitchen with her wet brush,
brushes off detectives with an open Dulux,
utters stories that dance your location,
faking an alibi stocked with disco lies. Coat
into an ending for Vera's guts. Your trail
froze its morgue, severe as winter levelled
at peeling George, murders tendered as
encore on failed paper. The sex workers
blade for canned punters, their patch
defended with bulletin and route pins. Boot
in for snow, a head in *The Yorkshire Post*
milked like coupons, mourning as sharp as
the light closing the neighbours' panes.
Your life is hanging its bat from grief: Peter
slogs his lorry over sun-gold moors, stoned
among light afternoons, clocks off for cod
beached on its peas as a Ramsden treat.
Peter's tally maroons him, itching in pubs:
he swells for cohorts of blue strippers who
goose the stage during January blasts.
Slates are blanked during the amnesty sleet.
Prostitutes agree to bait Lumb Lane: Peter is
saved by the game and the Mackem letter.

Yellow lightened in Manningham park as the bees trickled through a grill. Titus, marooned among the condoms, ripped from his town hall podium, dumped by the gates. Kids parked on the afternoon's edge, cadging for fags. Buzz Aldrin came, mumbled over the moon in school assembly as long as an Eagle's wake. Royal Standard: the spray quiffs rose high as the Silkerin, our first gig high on the penknife chubbed in pent jeans. The audience fell like clothes. A crew ducked the oak walls, cornered: Andy tacked, copped cobble lacerations, blooded into glaciers and a bathtub valley. Compensation like the city's iced excuse. She was fleeced with a cream footballer: her coat assumed his remaining seasons. I could bring her back in windows, mourning tapered, oblivious as school. Slashed case as a bullying charge: you were punched into an afternoon, spared for a trip. Jibes like clockwork until your muscles set: too gay for the team, according to Wisden. Revenge in a single wicket, a revved vulgarian ramping the snobs over roads for fun. Then recrimination: you were always the shirker, hammered unclubbable into a puff, crossing the country groans with jip when pitches froze the morning nights. Us slackers foxed into trees, backed by fags on the last circuit.

Unruly Patricia is the Tina's knees, fuzzy as custody. The Black Eyed Boys chart as you head for a punter in Lister Park, padded with industrial shadow, marooned around the old slabs. Men ghost Drummonds. Lads moon the windows as long as a 70s craze. Muzak builds into clients high on pants, wives doting on Chubby. Shout to the can, then on to more dives for mild, The Nash bombed into rubble on its stubborn plot. Unbutton the evening in a car's tube: worse for Tina with a muddy gob, ripe as a corner. Peter coaxes his Toyota through rain-lash to Lister's heights. Casual as a trench coat. The Carlisle's swing doors welcome you with gravy pints as Tina gips into a table. Cobbles lead into the valley, alley parade: you walk into the city's dogs, snibs panicked as kids race for a Whippy, fleeced with pops that belt into juice. Teenagers season into spots with Brew. Clocked into muscles, you grow into Jack, bulwarked as a pad. You bind a sheet, tight as Tina holds. You pillow her knees. You bring her back to the bedspread, arrange the rooms into charged vaults, then scram for a last Horlix. The groundsman shirks your hammer that you pitched into the Bingley gully. Estates settle to pints. Slacken into a Tetleys, monocled to a fox, backed into its last coop.

Crossleys: fists courted unhooked Becks
and stilettos knifed the stairwell in a club
where Friday barnies uncoupled the Soul.
Snogged mornings in backstreets cobbled
with aspirin where the mattresses flowered
descents from Northowram to black foam.
Spun down steps buttoned with frost, nights
ran too early into a retake churl. Stumped
after the last bus, top rocking sun in a daze,
upstairs like a cloud with ashtray stubs.
With cows after cash ran, Queensbury bog
where a mare smoked the dawn, stilt legs
awake to the sot. Locked out, defeated into
geranium heat and milk floating its electric,
the brambles cooling to bud. Verve in a cab
flooring its notch, dancing with ice dried to
the cooking solo. The ball turned and flared
its youth. A mill redesigned with vodka
hung the precipice: the club fired a night
and insurance dreams attached to a dad
knackered on the podium with till fingers.
A clown deposited his tongue before I could
desist, a cold ox wriggling neutered throat.
Then a late bus decked with homophobes:
chant rant at a polo neck clobbered in Zoot.
Lats scutted the bends, Ogden moss-dips:
benches peppered the moors, pubs trapped
in clientele, keys messed in shared trays,
addresses ungluing from faithful names.
Peas piled the leather slices meaty as gums.

You rubberneck cobbles as she circuits, clock the dandelions as you unhook your usual tool. A dog spins a lead onto clover as you cushion the dark. The mill oil runs into Josephine's body, clues as particles topped from a hammer. You are fitted as a fitter but Oldfield is a cloud dismissed by a crank who secretes B to lavish saliva, evisceration gummed to a V. Awake into fantasy, a Mackem lost in overheated data. Wakefield is electric for defeat, a chief brambled in tape hiss. His fingerprints sweat the plastic as an imposter tunes a ballad. Dolby notch in Yorkshire flats carry you through. You dice into silence, mill the questions cast as poker shots. Mallet dad brays your mum. His baby crimes: clowning gear in a shop; wiggling locks for fun on desultory rounds. He'd nick a crossbar if wasn't fastened; cars jack with bricks and uncoupled tyres. Peter bemoans shillings wasted on couples' beer. Mad as a lat, Carl blobs class, cultivates absence, dips a head into spat water and treacle peppered with bully spite. Coddled, you knuckle to a trapped school, abscond from Tong to a mess like a dinner plate: Colditz spliced into a Yorkshire barn. You rat on a farm, muck in a hen's beat and lift rabbits in a punch-net. Scrape your damage, the future spread like a cut in serial rations.

Ice doilies slide their bonnets: cars are inured to rain-lash. Sile interrupts breath, rank but pinned to a taxi fiver. Elizabeth sweats your palm to a squeeze. Please do not leave this mattress. A garage leaks its empty cars. Oil clouds scar the concrete. Sheepscar: Braine's *Room at the Top* settles among the dirty johns and Periplan binocs, slackening of flesh in these shebeen clubs, punters firing their hydrants and exiting up a club boarded with neglect, *Rainbow* arrow signing the entrance with misguided glee. Window gapes wet their upstairs cardboard: panes are brushed in to hide the seed, whitewashed to flake. A bulb fails its glow in a porn shop. A ballcock treats water as lava, flocked marble, chained desperation. A pilot light snickers, requires a blowtorch. Flats wasted as bricks point outside toilets still clenched to the last century. Snow. Once upon a glassed window, the synths record the time, punch and swill in a Sweda until you sign the nights. The storm halves day into purpose. Out of luck or money, you leave to milk your punters' round. It's a job: the middle class cannot understand that. This screwdriver head does not cam-out into verbals. The Philipps is liable to slip and can damage the screw. Pozidriv screwdrivers do not fit into a Phillips head.

A token of my affliction: a room swollen with leg. Convalescing punters exit night. Seeded in ashtrays, recovery takes the tea wetted in biscuits. You sully north to hide, unbulb your head. Thoughts must be pawned in a box room labelled to closet. Temperance Hall bathes its mist. Boys speak bass and repair to broken glasses. You can handle your shelf. There is salvation in the hob nobs chaining a couch. A skylight wastes Orion. Loving the illicit, Peter clenches a wheeze of the gear nicked in drawers crowing their blag. Was this it? Excursions mapped in a window as you clip your hair to the backstreet punch? You are a sign of the North, yet you purpose its sign. You leave your empathy on your motorbike on the carpet stairs: your iced mind applies your tools to Bradford's lashed districts. Wheel the size of Pudsey, a cabinet begins to revolve, to pin your fate. God came later. Sheepscar squeezes into leaked roads as cars empty pedestrians in Clay Pit Lane. Late pubs create lots drawn into exhaust and Peter's butter: lumber, cuttings, tips. Bread down for the night with a smash egg. You can do an operation after a salad: I wake to gassed verbals in Jimmy's as staff pump out the lingering aesthetic. Fix it. In broad sight, Peter fits into his corridor head.

NOTES

'WORTH'

The title of the first poem in this sequence, 'Manchester and Leeds – where are they?' is taken from Elizabeth Gaskell's biography of Charlotte Brontë. The whole sequence is, in a sense, a response to *The Life of Charlotte Brontë,* because Gaskell's book merges acute observations of mid-nineteenth-century Haworth and its environs with questionable accounts of the wild, vicious natives: Gaskell is rightly accused of perpetuating the 'Brontë myth' of the parsonage family growing up in the forgotten wastes of outer Yorkshire. Hence the sequence blends my own responses to the landscape and experiences of growing up in the region with direct quotations, and sometimes collages, from the biography, usually to subvert Gaskell's presumptions. In contrast, the first stanza of 'Manchester and Leeds – where are they?' presents a continuity between Gaskell's colourful 'larrups' and a landlord from Heptonstall who flitted while allegedly owing money to some regulars. Hence Gaskell's 'sleuth-hounds' pursuing their debts in the mid-nineteenth century cannot be completely disassociated from the concerns of the contemporary. The factory wheels at the end of the stanza refer, of course, to the industrialisation of the area in the nineteenth century compared to the previous domestic production of textiles, and the introduction of, for example, a cotton spinning shed in Hebden Bridge Mill.

One particular detail from the Gaskell biography that strikes me in the context of my own family history is Gaskell's characterisation of the dogged 'Norse' inhabitants. My own Bradford heritage takes the compass a little south: my family got into hairdressing in Essex before moving north (as I recount in my first poetry collection, *The Land of Green Ginger*); probably due to an outbreak of cholera in

London at the time. As a teenager, I worked for Bradford Council and emptied the bins in Haworth before partying at a house near the railway station on Bridgehouse Lane. Now my experiences of the village cannot be extricated from that of Gaskell's tourist, and yet I still cannot shake the mistaken sense that the Brontës were somehow 'ours'.

The sequence is also a form of creative redress: as a student, I was berated and excoriated in an essay for referring to the lack of curtains in the parsonage due to Patrick's worries over fires. Rewarded with several lines of red ink (it was that long ago) and critical invective, I was told that I was effectively contributing to the Brontë myth by peddling such nonsense. Thirty years later, I came across Professor Angus Easson's definitive annotations to *The Life of Charlotte Brontë*, which refer exactly to the lack of curtains in the parsonage. It is now time to draw a line under a pupil's simmering indignation.

'Caldebroc'

The Sagas of Icelanders informs this sequence. The opening poem, 'Swinton', alludes to the protagonist in 'Egil's Saga', the longest saga (182 pages in the Penguin edition).

In 'Norwegian Freeze', Kalf is a character from 'Grettir's Saga'.

'The Investment Manager's Report'

These poems refer to key figures in the financial crisis of 2008, and subsequent period of austerity. Fred Goodwin was the Chief Executive of the Royal Bank of Scotland between 2001 and 2009. It is alleged that he despised untidiness, to the extent that he had sloping filing cabinets designed, so that employees could not leave loose papers on top of them. Alan Greenspan was the Chair of the Federal Reserve in the USA (1987-2006). Philip Gramm is an American economist and politician.

'Urswick'

This sequence is dedicated to Richard Thomas Jones, who worked as a physical geographer at the University of Exeter. As 'Marl' recounts, his research contributed vastly to our understanding of what we now refer to as the Holocene. This poem refers to his memorial stone at Urswick Tarn in Cumbria, which records that his specialism was 'palaeo-environmental science, environmental pollution, natural archives and in the sharing of his knowledge with others. The importance of Urswick Tarn as a marl tarn of scientific significance, in addition to being a wildlife site of distinction, is affirmed by his work.'

'The Bingley Ripper'

Peter Sutcliffe, the so-called 'Yorkshire Ripper', grew up in Bingley, and lived for a while with Sonia and her parents in Clayton on the opposite side of the road to the housing estate where the author was a child at the time.

BIOGRAPHICAL NOTE

Antony Rowland has published three poetry collections: *The Land of Green Ginger* (Salt, 2008), *I Am a Magenta Stick* (Salt, 2012) and *M* (Arc, 2017). His poems were included in Roddy Lumsden's anthology *Identity Parade: New British and Irish Poets* (Bloodaxe, 2010).

Rowland received an Eric Gregory Award from the Society of Authors in 2000, and he was awarded the Manchester Poetry Prize in 2012. He was invited to record work for the UK Poetry Archive in 2009, and the Lyrikline (Germany) in 2014. The Dutch government elected him as a UK poetry 'ambassador' for 2016: his poetry was read on national television, and shown on screens at Schipol airport and Amsterdam Central Station.

In 2018, 'Newark' from *M* was shortlisted for the Forward Prize for Best Single Poem, and was published in *The Forward Book of Poetry 2019*. Peter Riley has described his work in *The Fortnightly Review* as 'an original and thoughtful handling of a major European modernist mode.'